PRESIDENT Barack
OBAMA
&
His Many
ACCOMPLISHMENTS

By Azaan Kamau

Glover Lane Press
Publishers Since January 2000
4570 Van Nuys Blvd Suite 573
Sherman Oaks, CA 91403
gloverlanepress@gmail.com
www.gloverlanepress.webs.com
Copyright © 2012 Glover Lane Press

Book Cover Design: Azaan Kamau of Glover Lane Press

The Mission of Glover Lane Press is to Uplift, Empower, Elevate the
Masses and Provide American Jobs. Every book published by
Glover Lane Press and it's many imprints, is printed and
manufactured in the United States of America, ensuring and
maintaining American employment.

Dedication

Dedicated to my Native American and
African Ancestors!

This work is also dedicated to the Barack Obama Presidential
Campaign for 2012. Thank you for your tireless work and
commitment.

Lastly, this book and all of its positive uplifting energy is dedicated
to the First Family;
President Obama, Michelle Obama and their two beautiful children!

Table of Contents

MORAL PRINCIPLES AND ETHICS

• Ordered the White House and all federal agencies to respect the Freedom of Information Act and overturned Bush-era limits on accessibility of federal documents (2009)

• Instructed all federal agencies to promote openness and transparency as much as possible (2009)

• Placed limits on lobbyists' access to the White House (2009)

• Placed limits on White House aides working for lobbyists after their tenure in the administration (2009)

• Signed a measure strengthening registration and reporting requirements for lobbyists (2009)

• Ordered that lobbyists must be removed from and are no longer permitted to serve on federal and White House advisory panels and boards (2009) * Note: After saying he would not hire lobbyists, a few have been hired in the Administration

• Companies and individuals who are delinquent on their taxes or owe back taxes are no longer allowed to bid for federal contracts (2009)

• Initiated the "e-Rulemaking Initiative" (in cooperation with Cornell University) to allow for online public "notice and comment" of federal laws and initiatives (2010)

• Issued the "Open Gov Directive" ordering all Cabinet departments to promote transparency and citizen participation in their policies (2010)

• Signed extensions on banning lobbyists from serving on agency boards (2010)

EDUCATION

• Authorized construction funds for high-speed, broadband Internet access in K-12 public schools (2009)

• Increased funding for school construction (2009)

• Increased funding available for student loans (2009)

• Expanded the national youth service program (2009)

• Streamlined the federal student loan process to save $87 billion over the next 10 years (2009)

• Changed the rule to allow students struggling to make college loan payments to refinance their loans (2009)

• Beginning discussions with Congress for education reform (2009)
* Note: Much of Obama's education reform has been sidelined by opposition in Congress

• Initiated a "Race to the Top" competitive federal grant program for states who develop innovative policies (2009)

• Instituted a "judgment review" allowing families with student loans to petition to have their current financial status determine the loan rather than the previous year's finances (2009)

• Launched "Educate to Innovate," a public/private partnership making $236 million available for science, mathematics, and technology education programs (2009)

• Proposed capping the maximum amount students must pay on student loans (as percentage of their income) (2010)

• Proposed reducing student loan obligations for individuals going to work in community and public service jobs (2010)

• The federal government will offer direct student loans, cutting out the cost of private banks ("middle man") who increase the costs in order to make a profit (2010)

• Increased investment in technologies for schools/education (2010)

ENERGY & ENVIRONMENT

• Offered attractive tax write-offs for those who buy hybrid automobiles (2009)

• Overturned Bush-era rule that weakened the Endangered Species Act (2009)

• Announced plans to purchase fuel efficient American-made fleet for the federal government (2009)

• Ended the Bush-era policy of not regulating and labeling carbon dioxide emissions (2009)

• Signed a measure requiring energy producing plants to begin producing 15% of their energy from renewable sources (2009)

• Announced that the federal government would reengage in the long-delayed effort to clean up "Superfund" toxic waste sites (2009)

• Announced the long-term development of a national energy grid with renewable sources and cleaner, efficient energy production (2009) * Note: Much of Obama's energy reform was killed by Senate Republicans

• Proposed a new refuge for wild mustangs (2009)

• Cancelled several Bush-era mountain-top removal and mining permits (2009)

• Reengaged in international treaties and agreements to protect the Antarctic (2009)

* Note: Bush had withdrawn from such efforts

• Asked Congress for an energy reform and "cap and trade" bill (2009) * Note: The Congress failed to pass such a bill

• Developing plan to lease US coastal waters for wind and water-current energy production (2009)

• Overturned Bush-era policies that allowed uranium mining near national parks such as the Grand Canyon (2009)

• Expanded the Petrified Forest National Park (2009)

• Signed the Omnibus Public Lands Management Act that protects millions of acres of scenic, historic, and recreational lands and trails (2009)

• Required that government buildings and facilities be retrofitted to save energy costs (2009) * Note: These green retrofits are moving very slowly

• Authorized studies in several western states to determine how to support large-scale solar installations (2009)

• Attended the Copenhagen talks and, after the talks were stalled, negotiated an international (voluntary) agreement on reducing carbon emissions and raising funds to assist developing nations in offsetting carbon emissions (2009)

• Banned importation of pythons in response to a growing population of pythons damaging the Florida Everglades (2009)

• Committing the federal government to increasing research and use of renewable, clean energy sources such as wind, biomass, etc. (2009)

• Executive orders establishing a federal initiative to reduce greenhouse gas emissions in all federal operations (2009) (2010)

• Agreed to consider increases in nuclear energy production and requested a study on the feasibility of nuclear power plant construction (2010) * Note: Nearly all energy initiatives were defeated by Republican opposition in Congress

• Increased investment in clean energy projects (2010)

• Executive Order to develop a new strategy for and commitment to ocean and lake resources, and for scientific research on water quality (2010)

DISASTER RESPONSE

• Ordered a review of hurricane and natural disaster preparedness (2009)

• FEMA once again reports directly to the president (2009) * Note: Bush removed FEMA (prior to the Hurricane Katrina disaster) from this status

• Demonstrated an immediate and efficient response to the floods in North Dakota and other natural disasters (2009)

• Ordered that funds be released and red tape be streamlined for the ongoing Hurricane Katrina recovery effort in the Gulf Coast (2009)

• Timely response to the January 2010 earthquake and ensuing humanitarian crisis (2010)

Components of the response:

- The FBI's National Center for Disaster Fraud was tasked to look into possible fraud with organizations soliciting funds for relief

- Announced the Clinton-Bush Haiti Fund

- Established an emergency Haiti Task Force in the State Department

- Established a website with information, resources, and a posting of a "person finder" online to help families and friends to locate loved ones

- Joint aid and relief planning with the U.K.

- Sponsored a resolution in the UN Security Council for additional security and police forces in Haiti

- Dispatched the US Navy floating hospital (USNS Comfort) and, within 5 days, 9 naval and relief ships, 5 Coast Guard cutters, 8 Coast Guard aircraft, and 12,000 US military personnel

- Initial dispatch of several ships and cargo planes full of humanitarian aid and supplies, 6 search/rescue teams (500 personnel), and 265 Department of Health & Human Services personnel for emergency medical and aid support

- Established a mobile US air traffic control center at the destroyed airport in Port-au-Prince

• After the BP Deepwater Horizon oil spill in the Gulf of Mexico, a freeze was placed on new deep water projects (2010)

• Executive Order to establish new security measures to minimize accidental release of bio and chemical agents; new strategies for public health and bioterrorism response (2010)

• Established a national commission on the BP Deepwater Horizon spill to examine facts and report a plan of action; new efforts to prevent offshore spills (2010)

• After a slow start in responding to the BP Deepwater Horizon oil spill, the White House is promoting a long-term plan to reconstruct the damaged Gulf and negotiated with BP the establishment of a multi-billion dollar trust fund for victims of the spill (2010)

• Extended national flood insurance program for those in need during current economic crisis (2010)

FOREIGN POLICY

• Closed the Bush-era "secret detention" facilities in Eastern Europe (2009)

• Ended the Bush-era policy allowing "enhanced interrogation" (torture); the US is again in compliance with Geneva Convention standards (2009) * Note: Obama has permitted some controversial interrogation techniques to continue

• Restarted international nuclear non-proliferation talks and reestablished international nuclear inspection protocols (2009) * Note: Bush withdrew from non-proliferation talks and dismantled the inspection infrastructure

• Reengaged in the treaties/agreements to protect the Antarctic (2009) * Note: These were suspended under Bush

• Reengaged in the agreements/talks on global warming and greenhouse gas emissions (2009) * Note: These were suspended under Bush

• Visited more countries and met with more world leaders than any president in his first six months in office (2009)

• Banned the export of cluster bombs (2009)

• Overturned Bush-era plans to increase the US nuclear arsenal (2009)

• Authorized the Navy SEALS operation that freed by force the US shipping captain held by Somali pirates (2009)

• Restored the US commitment to the UN population fund for family planning; overturned the ban on providing funds internationally for family planning (2009) * Note: The family planning efforts were suspended under Bush

• Instituted a new policy on Cuba, allowing Cuban families to return "home" to visit families (2009)

• Extended an offer of engagement (free from sanctions and penalties) to Iran through December 31, 2009 (Iran did not accept the offer) (2009)

• Sent envoys to the Middle East and other parts of the world, reengaging in multilateral and bilateral talks and diplomacy (2009)

• Authorized discussions with North Korea and the private mission by former president, Bill Clinton, to secure the release of two Americans held in prisons (2009)

• Authorized discussions with Myanmar and the mission by Senator Jim Web to secure the release of an American held captive (2009)

• Renewed loan guarantees for Israel (2009)
• Signed the USIFTA trade agreement with/for Israel (2009)

• Authorized a $550m advance for Israel (six months prior to the scheduled date) in order to accommodate Israeli's economic and financial needs (2009)

• Continued agreements with Israel for cultural exchanges, immigration, etc. (2009)

• Spoke on Arab television, spoke at an Egyptian university, and met with Arab leaders in an effort to change the tone of US-Arab relations (2009)

• Ordered the US to finally pay its dues to the United Nations (2009)

• Attended the Summit of America's meeting in Trinidad and Tobago (2010)

• Dispatched several envoys and initiated talks with numerous nations (2010)

• Signed a nuclear limitation treaty with Russia (2010) * Note: The agreement calls for both countries to reduce their nukes by one-third (1,500) and launch systems by half (800)

• Hosted nuclear non-proliferation summit for several nations (2010)

• Executive Order to establish support offices in the State Department to assist the governments of Pakistan and Afghanistan (2010)

• Presidential Memoranda to continue drug interdiction support with Columbia (2010)

THE WHITE HOUSE

• The White House website now provides information on all economic stimulus projects and spending, along with an unprecedented amount of information on our government (2009)

• Ended the Bush-era practice of circumventing established FDA rules for political reasons (2009)

• Ended the Bush-era practice of having White House staff rewrite the findings of scientific and environmental regulations and reports when they disagreed with the results (2009)

• Limited the salaries of senior White House aides (salaries cut to $100,000) (2009)

• Has urged Congress to adopt "Pay-Go" (whereby each dollar of spending is offset by a dollar in cuts or revenues, which was used in the `90s but abandoned in the `00s) (2010)
• Has been holding open meetings with Republican leaders, although they complain of a lack of access and information (2010)

• Signed the Improper Payments Elimination and Recovery Act (2010) * Note: To curb wasteful spending

• Tasked federal agencies to develop plans for disposing of unneeded real estate and then to eliminate unnecessary or non-economical lands, properties, etc. (2010)

NATIONAL SECURITY

• Phasing out the expensive F-22 war plane (which wasn't even used in Iraq/Afghanistan) and other outdated weapons systems (2009)

• Announced his intention to close the detention facility at Guantanamo Bay (2009) * Note: The closure has been delayed due to massive opposition but it remains on the agenda.

• Stated his interest in housing terrorists at a new federal "super max" facility in the US (2009) * Note: this has been delayed in the face of massive opposition but it remains on the agenda

• Cut the expensive Reagan era missile defense program, saving $1.4 billion in 2010 (2009)

• Cancelled plans to station anti-ballistic missile systems in Poland and the Czech Republic (2009)

• Replaced long-range, expensive missile systems with more efficient smaller systems (2009)

• Increased US Navy patrols off the Somali coast in response to pirating (2009)

• Established a new cyber-security office and appointed a cyber-security czar (2009)

• Ordered the first nation-wide comprehensive cyber threat assessment (2009)

• Instituted a new Nuclear Posture Review, revising US nuclear deterrence policy to encourage more nations to join the 1996 Comprehensive Test Ban Treaty (2010) * Note: Components of the policy include: a pledge to stop nuclear testing; a pledge to not build a new generation of nukes; identifying nuclear terrorism, rather than a launch from another nuclear state, as the major threat; a pledge to not use nukes on a non-nuclear state in a conventional conflict; etc.

• Executive orders to block payment, transfers, exports, etc... of individuals and organizations support the regimes of North Korea, Iran, Somali pirates, and other foreign threats (2010)

• Presidential Memoranda to extend certain provisions of The Trading with Enemies Act which was to expire in September 2010 (2010) * Note: This includes freezing assets and banning trade that benefits the Cuban regime; however further efforts at normalizing travel to Cuba are supported

• Signed bill for southwest border security and increased funds and agents on the Mexican border (2010)

• Signed the Comprehensive Sanctions, Accountability and Divestment Act to deal with foreign regimes like Iran and North Korea (2010)

ECONOMY

• Increased infrastructure spending (roads, bridges, power plants…) (2009) * Note: Bush was the first president since Herbert Hoover to not make infrastructure a priority

• Authorized the US auto industry rescue plan and two GMAC rescue packages (2009)

• Authorized the housing rescue plan and new FHA residential housing guarantees (2009)

• Authorized a $789 billion economic stimulus plan (2009) * Note: 1/3 in tax cuts for working-class families; 1/3 to states for infrastructure projects; 1/3 to states to prevent the layoff of police officers, teachers, etc. at risk of losing their jobs because of state budget shortfalls

• Instituted a new rule allowing the public to meet with federal housing insurers to refinance (in as quickly as one day) a mortgage if they are having trouble paying (2009)

• Authorized a continuation of the US financial and banking rescue plans initiated at the end of the Bush administration and authorized TARP funds to buy "toxic assets" from failing financial institutions (2009)

• Authorized the "Cash for Clunkers" program that stimulated auto sales and removed old, inefficient, polluting cars from the road (2009)

• Convened a "jobs summit" to bring experts together to develop ideas for creating jobs (2009)

• Ordered the FDIC to beef up deposit insurance (2009)

• Ended the Bush-era policy of protecting credit card companies (2009) * Note: In place of the old policy, new consumer protections were instituted and the industry's predatory practices were banned

• Authorized the federal government to make more loans available to small businesses and ordered lower rates for federal loans to small businesses (2009)

• Placed a 35% tariff on Chinese tires and a few other products such as pipes after China was found to be illegally "dumping" exports below cost (2009) * Note: Clinton, Bush I, and Reagan all refused to "get tough" on China's predatory trade practices; Bush II refused four times during his presidency

• Called on Congress to deliver a "Jobs bill" (2010)

• Credit card companies are prohibited from raising rates without advance notification or arbitrarily if customers are paying bills on time (2010)

• Signed a bill to extend unemployment benefits set to expire (2010)

• Signed historic Wall Street reform bill (2010) * Note: Designed to re-regulate and end abusive practices and promote consumer protections

• Signed the HIRE Act to stimulate the economic recovery (2010) * Note: The bill includes: tax cuts for small businesses who hire someone unemployed for at least two months; small businesses can write off their investments in equipment this year; etc.

• National Export Initiative established to enhance federal support (technical assistance, training, trade missions, etc.) and coordination efforts to help US businesses export products and services (2010)

• Initiatives to promote a "Wireless Broadband Revolution" (2010) * Note: Among other things, broadband is finally being considered as necessary infrastructure, with efforts to expand use, access, and spectrum...

• Expanded agricultural credit to farmers during current economic crisis (2010)

• Signed bill - US Manufacturing Enhancement Act (2010)

• Signed bill - Single Family Housing Mortgage Insurance (2010)

TAXES

• Negotiated a deal with Swiss banks to permit the US government to gain access to records of tax evaders and criminals (2009)

• Ended the Bush-era policy of offering tax benefits to corporations who outsource American jobs (2009) * Note: The new policy promotes in-sourcing investments to brings jobs back to the US

• Signed the American Recovery and Reinvestment Act which provides small tax cuts for 95% of "working families" (2009) * Note: The tax cuts were not as big as was suggested during the 2008 campaign

• Convened an advisory board that is looking into simplifying the tax code (2009)

• Ordered the closing of offshore tax safe havens (for individual and business tax evaders) (2009)
• Reduced taxes for some small businesses to stimulate the economic recovery (2009)

• Extended the Home Buyers Credit for first-time home buyers (2009)

• Proposed doubling the child tax credit (2010)

• Called for the repeal of the capital gains tax for small businesses (2010)

• Proposed rolling back the 2001 and 2003 Bush tax cuts for the wealthiest Americans (2010) * Note: This would be for families earning over $250,000/year and would return their tax rates to the 1990's level

THE BUDGET

• Ordered all federal agencies to undertake a study and make recommendations for ways to cut federal spending (2009)

• Ordered a review of all federal operations to identify wasteful spending and practices (2009)

• Established a National Performance Officer charged with saving the federal government money and making federal operations more efficient (2009)

• Overturned the Bush-era practice of not listing certain federal programs in the federal budget (2009) (2010) * Note: Bush did this (so did Reagan) in an effort to hide programs and make the budget look smaller; such "off budget" items are now included in the annual budget

• Full appropriations for war are now included in the budget (2009) (2010) * Note: Bush did not list many of the appropriations for Iraq, Afghanistan, and War on Terror

• Funds for emergency appropriations are now included in the budget (2009) (2010)

• Proposed a three-year freeze on federal discretionary spending beginning in 2011 (2010)

• Is in the process of cutting 120 federal programs identified as either wasteful or unnecessary (2010)

• Established a bipartisan commission on fiscal responsibility, staffed by House and Senate members and private citizens, tasked with submitting proposals to balance the budget (2010) * Note: In the face of Republican opposition, the powers of the commission were watered down

• Established a bipartisan commission on the future of Social Security, tasked with submitting proposals to preserve and strengthen Social Security (2010) * Note: In the face of Republican opposition, the powers of the commission were watered down

• Cut $20 billion from federal budget and has pledged to cut at least this much every year (2010)

• Ultimately decided to cancel planned new presidential helicopter fleet and stick with Marine One (2010)

• Freezing all discretionary spending for next three years, except on national security (2010)

• Presidential Memoranda to freeze discretionary awards, bonuses, etc. for federal political appointees (2010)

• Beginning to use "Pay-As-You-Go" (Pay-Go) to offset budget expenditures with budget cuts or revenue enhancements (2010)

IRAQ & AFGHANISTAN

• Began the phased withdrawal of US troops from Iraq (2009); continuing the withdrawal (2010)

• Changed the US military command in the Afghan conflict (2009)

• Tasked the Pentagon to reorganize US policy in Afghanistan; the new policy includes 30,000 additional troops deployed, priority training of Afghan forces, developing agriculture and infrastructure, limiting aerial bombing, etc. (2009)

• Ordered the Pentagon to send additional helicopters to assist US Marine units and Special Forces in Afghanistan (2009)

• Increased unmanned drone strikes on Taliban and al-Qaeda targets in Afghanistan (2009)

• Ended the Bush-era "stop-loss" policy that kept soldiers in Iraq/Afghanistan longer than their enlistment date (2009)

VETERANS & ARMED FORCES

• Ended the Bush-era "blackout" imposed on media coverage of the return of fallen US soldiers (2009) * Note: The media is now permitted to cover the story pending adherence to respectful rules and with the approval of the fallen soldier's family

• Ended the Bush-era "black out" policy on media coverage of war casualties (2009) * Note: Full information is now released for the first time in the War on Terror

• Ordered better body armor to be procured for US troops (2009)

• Funding new Mine Resistant Ambush Vehicles (2009) * Note: The old Hummers were very vulnerable to roadside explosives and an alarming percentage of our soldiers lost in Iraq were on account of IEDs

• Working to increase pay and benefits for military personnel (2009)

• Improving housing for military personnel (2009)

• Initiating a new policy to promote federal hiring of military spouses (2009)

• Ordered that conditions at Walter Reed Military Hospital and other neglected military hospitals be improved (2009)

• Beginning the process of reforming and restructuring the military to a post-Cold War, modern fighting force (2009) * Note: Bush announced in 2001 his intention to do this but backed off the reforms after 9/11, which include: new procurement policies; increasing the size of Special Ops units; deploying new technologies; creating new cyber security units; etc.

• Ended the Bush-era practice of awarding "no-bid" defense contracts (2009)

• Improving benefits for veterans as well as VA staffing, information systems, etc. (2009)

• Authorized construction of additional health centers to care for veterans (2009)

• Suspended the Bush-era decision to purchase a fleet of Marine One helicopters from suppliers in favor of American made helicopters (2009)

• Ordered a review of the existing "Don't ask, don't tell" policy on gays in the military (2010)

• New GI Bill for returning veterans from Iraq and Afghanistan (2009)

• Signed bill providing assistance for caregivers of veterans wounded in Iraq and Afghanistan (2010) * Note: The omnibus bill does the following: Training, funding, and counseling for caregivers; promoting pilot childcare programs for women vets under treatment at the VA; independent oversight to prevent abuse; readjustment counseling for National Guard and reservist units; etc.

• Eliminated co-payments for veterans who are catastrophically disabled (2010)

• Fulfilled campaign promise to have combat troops (90,000) out of Iraq by August 31, 2010 (2010)

• Established a new interagency task force to assist veterans owning small businesses (2010) * Note: The efforts include promoting federal contract opportunities, improve access to loans and capital, mentor assistance programs, etc.

HUMAN RIGHTS

• Instituted enforcements for equal pay for women (Lilly Ledbetter Act) (2009)

• Appointed Sonia Sotomayor, the first Latina, to the Supreme Court (2009)

• Held the first Seder in White House (2009)

• Appointed a diverse Cabinet and diverse White House staff (2009)

• Spoke at the annual dinner of the Human Rights Campaign, a gay rights organization (2009)

• Signed the first major piece of federal gay rights legislation that includes acts of violence against gays under the list of federal hate crimes (2009)

• Reversed the Bush-era practice of politicizing Justice Department investigations and prosecutions against political opponents (2009)

• Pushing for some of the 9/11 perpetrators to be tried in federal court (2009) * Note: The process has moved at a snail's pace and, in the face of opposition, Obama has remained quiet

• Signed an extension of the Ryan White HIV/AIDS Treatment Bill to provide federal research and support for treating the disease (2009)

• Allowed the State Department of offer same-sex benefits for employees (2009)

• Proposed that the Pentagon repeal the "Don't Ask, Don't Tell" policy; placed a "freeze" on current efforts to remove alleged homosexuals from the military (2009)

• After eight years of neglect, the Justice Department and EEOC are again enforcing employment discrimination laws (2009)

• Convened the White House Tribal Nations Conference, inviting representatives from 564 federally-recognized Indian tribes (2009)

• Provided increased school projects for Indian lands and increased funds for the Indian Health Service (2009)

• Signed an Executive Order mandating that his Cabinet develop plans to work with and consult Indian tribes on issues impacting Indian lands (2009)

• Commissioned a study to develop alternatives to "Don't Ask, Don't Tell" (2010)

• Called for federal agencies to look into recognizing gay partnerships in terms of benefits (2010)
• Signed an Executive Order for the President's Initiative on Historically Black Colleges and Universities (2010)

• Increased funding for Historically Black Colleges and Universities (2010)

• Signed Executive Order to promote the federal government as a "model employer" when it comes to hiring the disabled (2010) * Note: This includes new efforts to increase recruitment, hiring, and training for the disabled

• Programs to assist Spanish speakers with the US Census (2010)

• Elena Kagen appointed to Supreme Court (2010)

• Tasked all federal agencies to develop new strategies to address HIV/AIDS (2010)

• After organizing studies on the topic in 2009, tasked the Pentagon to eliminate "Don't Ask, Don't Tell" (2010)

• Signed Fair Sentencing Act (2010) * Note: The Administration continues to deescalate marijuana interdiction and raids; increased dramatically the amount of cocaine one must possess to be sentenced to jail; eliminated mandatory sentencing for first-time drug abusers and simple possession.

HEALTHCARE

• Removed Bush era restrictions on embryonic stem-cell research (2009)

• Federal support for stem-cell and new biomedical research (2009)

• Expanded the SCHIP program to cover health care for 4 million more children (2009)

• Established an independent commission to make recommendations on slowing the costs of Medicare (2009)

• Reversed some of the Bush-era restrictions that prevented Medicare from negotiating with pharmaceutical firms for cheaper drugs, allowing government to again competitively bid (2009) * Note: Obama had promised to lift all restrictions but, while he did negotiate with drug companies for them to lower their costs the deal only lifted some restrictions

• Expanding government vaccination programs (2009)

• Issued new disease prevention guidelines and priorities for the CDC (2009)

• Authorized the FDA to finally begin regulating tobacco (2009)

• Tasked federal labs to prioritize research on and deployment of H1N1 vaccines (2009)

• Asked multiple congressional committees to bring forward a healthcare reform bill; held dozens of public hearings and town halls on the issue (2009) (2010)

• Established a new council on National Prevention, Health Promotion, and Public Health to be chaired by Surgeon General and charged with promoting healthy lifestyles and integrative healthcare (2010)

• When accusations to the contrary arose, an Executive Order was signed to reaffirm that federal funds are not to be used for abortion services (2010)

• Historic healthcare reform bill signed - $940 billion over 10 years (2010) * Note: 32 million additional Americans will receive healthcare coverage and costs will be lowered for most Americans, but many of the goals are phased in over four years.

Components of the bill

- Prevents insurance companies from denying coverage to individuals/family members with pre-existing health conditions; a temporary plan is being developed to cover high-risk individuals with pre-existing conditions until the full reforms go into effect in 2014

- Prevents insurance companies from placing lifetime limits on benefits

- An individual's out-of-pocket healthcare expenses are capped

- Closes the "donut hole" (Part D) for Medicare prescription drug coverage (under Bush, Medicare helped pay for drugs up to $2,600 and above $4,550, but individuals had to pay 100% of the costs in between these amounts); now Medicare helps cover costs irrespective of the amount – seniors will now pay only 25% of drug costs up to $4,550 and only 5% of drug costs above that amount

- In 2010, an emergency provision will offer seniors a $250 rebate on the costs incurred within the "donut hole"

- Individuals living at or below the poverty line were eligible for healthcare under Medicaid, but by 2014 individuals/families living slightly above (making up to $14,404/$29,327) the poverty line will also be eligible for benefits

- Individuals/families making less than $43,320/$88,200 per year will qualify for government subsidies to help purchase health insurance

- All individuals must have health insurance or face a government fine; all large (over 50 employees) employers must offer health insurance to employees or pay a fine

- Small businesses can get a tax credit if they offer health care

- There are hardship exemptions if individuals can't afford health insurance

- Families can keep their children in college on their plans through age 26

- Promotes health insurance "exchanges" so consumers can buy "wholesale"

- Creates consumer assistance offices to help consumers file complaints or appeal decisions from insurance companies; beginning in 2011, insurance companies can no longer make excessive rate hikes without justification and approval, and those doing so may be barred from participating in new health insurance exchanges

Funding sources:

- Large employers (over 50 workers) that don't offer health benefits will be charged a $2,000/worker fee; if the employer offers coverage but employees instead purchase federally subsidized insurance the fee is $3,000/worker receiving federal subsidies or $750/worker (whichever is lower)

- Annual fees on pharmaceutical companies ($27 billion), health insurance companies ($60 billion), and medical device-makers ($20 billion)

- Annual penalties on individuals who do not have health insurance (up to a maximum of $695/person)

- Increase in the Medicare payroll tax from 1.45% to 2.35% for individuals making $200,000+ and families making $250,000+

- 3.8% tax on unearned income for millionaires
- Insurance companies will be subject to a tax on each high-end insurance plan (so-called "Cadillac" plans) they offer.

SGL/ LGBTq

FEDERAL LEGISLATION SIGNED INTO LAW

- Signed the Matthew Shepard and James Byrd, Jr. Hate Crimes Prevention Act, which expanded existing United States federal hate crime law to include crimes motivated by a victim's actual or perceived gender, sexual orientation, gender identity, or disability -- the first positive federal LGBT legislation in the nation's history

- Repealed Don't Ask/Don't Tell

- Signed the Ryan White HIV/AIDS Treatment Extension Act.

POLICIES CHANGED

- Reversed US refusal to sign the UN Declaration on Sexual Orientation and Gender Identity
- Extended benefits to same-sex partners of federal employees in 2009 and, further, in 2010
- Lifted the HIV Entry Ban
- Issued diplomatic passports, and provided other benefits, to the partners of same-sex foreign service employees
- Committed to ensuring that federal housing programs are open to all, regardless of sexual orientation or gender identity
- Conceived a National Resource Center for Lesbian, Gay, Bisexual and Transgender Elders -- the nation's first ever -- funded by a three-year HHS grant to SAG
- Banned job discrimination based on gender identity throughout the Federal government (the nation's largest employer)
- Eliminated the discriminatory Census Bureau policy that kept same-sex relationships from being counted, encouraging couples who consider themselves married to file that way, even if their state of residence does not yet permit legal marriage
- Instructed HHS to require any hospital receiving Medicare or Medicaid funds (virtually all hospitals) to allow LGBT visitation rights
- Required all grant applicants seeking HUD funding to comply with state and local anti-discrimination laws that protect LGBT individuals
- Adopted transgender recommendations on the issuance of gender-appropriate passports that will ease barriers to safe travel and that will provide government-issued ID that avoids involuntary "outing" in situations requiring ID, like hiring, where a gender-appropriate driver's license or birth certificate is not available
- Extended domestic violence protections to LGBT victims

- Extended the Family and Medical Leave Act to cover employees taking unpaid leave to care for the children of same-sex partners
- Issued guidance to assist tenants denied housing on the basis of sexual orientation or gender identity and banned LGBT discrimination in all HUD-assisting housing and HUD-assisted loans
- Issued a National HIV/AIDS Strategy praised as "long-overdue" by the Task Force, Lambda and others
- Issued guidance to 15,000 local departments of education and 5,000 colleges to support educators in combating bullying
- Cut back authority to discharge under Don't Ask/Don't Tell from hundreds of generals to just 6 civilian appointees, effectively ending discharges while working toward a permanent end to the policy.
- Launched the first-ever national study of discrimination against members of the LGBT community in the rental and sale of housing
- Determined that Section 3 of DOMA is unconstitutional
- Determined that LGBT discrimination should be subject to a standard of "heightened scrutiny"
- Stopped defending DOMA, leading to "dramatic changes across the country and the federal government in the way that lawyers and judges see legal challenges brought by LGBT people - and, slowly but surely, in the way that LGBT people are able to live their lives"
- Filed an unprecedented brief detailing the history of discrimination faced by gay, lesbian and bisexual people in America, including by the federal government itself -- the single most persuasive legal argument ever advanced by the United States government in support of equality for lesbian, gay and bisexual people
- Vacated a court order that would have deported a gay American's Venezuelan partner
- Began recognizing joint bankruptcy petitions filed by same-sex married couples
- Endorsed the Respect for Marriage Act
- Reduced the deportation threat faced by binational LGBT couples

- Authorized military chaplains to perform same-sex weddings on or off military bases
- Upped the nation's commitment to fighting HIV/AIDS at home and abroad
- Launched a muscular, game-changing campaign for global LGBT equality, highlighted by the Secretary of State in a half-hour address to the United Nations
- Extended the gender-based employment discrimination protections of the 1964 Civil Rights Act to transgender employees
- Added an LGBT representative to the diversity program at each of the nations 120 federal prisons.

RESPECT & INCLUSION

- Endorsed the Baldwin-Lieberman bill, The Domestic Partnership Benefits and Obligations Act of 2009, to provide FULL partnership benefits to federal employees
- Released the first Presidential PRIDE proclamations since 2000
- Hosted the first LGBT Pride Month Celebration in White House history
- Awarded the Presidential Medal of Freedom to Harvey Milk and Billie Jean King, joining past recipients such as Rosa Parks
- Appointed the first ever transgender DNC member
- Testified in favor of ENDA, the first time any official of any administration has testified in the Senate on ENDA
- Hired more openly LGBT officials (like these) in its first two years -- more than 150, including more than 20 "Senate-confirmable" -- than any previous administration hired in four years or eight
- Sworn in Ambassador David Huebner
- Changed the culture of government everywhere from – among others – HUD and HHS to the Export-Import Bank, the State Department, and the Department of Education
- Appointed Justices Sonia Sotomayor and Elena Kagan, instead of conservatives who would have tilted the Court even further to the right and virtually doomed our rights for a generation.
- Named open transgender appointees (the first President ever to do so)
- Emphasized LGBT inclusion in everything from the President's historic NAACP address ("The pain of discrimination is still felt in America. By African American women paid less for doing the same work as colleagues of a different color and a different gender. By Latinos made to feel unwelcome in their own country. By Muslim Americans viewed with suspicion simply because they kneel down to pray to their God. By our gay brothers and sisters, still taunted, still attacked, still denied their rights.") . . . to the first paragraph of his Family Day proclamation ("Whether

children are raised by two parents, a single parent, grandparents, a same-sex couple, or a guardian, families encourage us to do our best and enable us to accomplish great things") and his Mothers Day proclamation ("Nurturing families come in many forms, and children may be raised by two parents, a single mother, two mothers, a step-mom, a grandmother, or a guardian. Mother's Day gives us an opportunity to celebrate these extraordinary caretakers") . . . to creating the chance for an adorable 10-year-old at the White House Easter Egg roll to tell ABC World News how cool it is to have two mommies . . . to including the chair of the National Gay and Lesbian Chamber of Commerce along with the Secretary of the Treasury and the President of Goldman Sachs in the small audience for the President's economic address at the New York Stock Exchange . . . to welcoming four gay couples to its first State Dinner

- Recommitted, in a televised address, to passing ENDA . . . repealing Don't Ask/Don't Tell . . . repealing the so-called Defense of Marriage Act
- Spoken out against discrimination at the National Prayer Breakfast ("We may disagree about gay marriage, but surely we can agree that it is unconscionable to target gays and lesbians for who they are -- whether it's here in the United States or, as Hillary mentioned, more extremely in odious laws that are being proposed most recently in Uganda.")
- Dispatched the Secretary of Defense and the Chairman of the Joint Chiefs of Staff to call on the Senate to repeal Don't Ask / Don't Tell
- Launched a website to gather public comment on first-ever federal LGBT housing discrimination study
- Appointed long-time equality champion Chai Feldblum one of the four Commissioners of the Equal Employment Opportunity Commission
- Produced U.S. Census Bureau PSAs featuring gay, lesbian, and transgender spokespersons
- Appointed Retired Colonel Margarethe Cammermeyer, an early public champion of open service in the military, to the Defense Advisory Committee on Women in the Services

- Successfully fought for UN accreditation of IGLHRC (the International Gay & Lesbian Human Rights Commission) -- against Republican attempts to block it
- Convened the first-ever anti-bullying summit to craft a national strategy to reduce bullying in schools
- Launched stopbullying.gov
- Awarded $13.3 million to the LA Gay & Lesbian Center to create a model program for LGBTQ youth in the foster care system
- Tweeted to 5.7 million @BarackObama followers and nearly 2 million @WhiteHouse followers the President's "It Gets Better" video
- Embraced that campaign with heartfelt messages from, as well, the Vice President, the Secretary of State, the Secretary of Agriculture (aimed particularly at rural youth), the Secretaries of Education and Health & Human Services, the Secretary of Labor (in English and Spanish), the Director of OPM and LGBT members of the White House staff
- Issued a Department of Justice video urging kids to call a Justice Department toll-free number if their school is aware of bullying but taking no action
- Held the first ever White House conference on bullying prevention, led by the President and First Lady
- Hosted first-ever White House transgender policy meeting
- Emphasized the positive value of Gay-straight Student Alliances (GSAs) and advised the nation's school districts of their legal responsibility to allow establishment of GSAs
- Appointed the first openly gay man to serve on the federal bench
- Nominated the first out lesbian US attorney
- Nominated the first openly gay US attorney to serve Texas
- Forced the Tehachipi Unified School District to prevent and respond to gender-based harassment
- Acknowledged in federal court the U.S. government's "significant and regrettable role" in discrimination in America against gays and lesbians, arguing that DOMA is unconstitutional. ("This is your U.S. Justice Department, folks, forcefully, stunningly taking on the homophobes in Congress and a huge Obama WIN." -- Rex Wockner)

- Appointed open lesbian activist to West Point advisory board
- Used the President's annual United Nations address to say, "no country should deny people their rights because of who they love, which is why we must stand up for the rights of gays and lesbians everywhere."
- Presented Janice Langbehn with the Presidential Citizens Award for her role in securing hospital visitation rights
- Convened the first-ever White House LGBT Elder Housing summit
- Endorsed the Student Non-Discrimination Act and the Safe Schools improvement Act targeting discrimination and bullying based on sexual orientation and gender identity
- Endorsed marriage equality

THE INITIATIVES

• New federal funding for science and research labs (2009)

• Signed national service legislation; expanded national youth service program (2009)

• Increasing opportunities in AmeriCorps program (2009)

• Instituted a new focus on mortgage fraud (2009)

• Ordered the DEA to stop raids on medical marijuana usage (2009)

• Ordered a review of existing "mandatory minimum" prison sentencing (2009)

• Signed an order to limit airport tarmac delays and the time passengers had to sit in the plane/on the tarmac during delays (2009)

• Restored the EPA to "Cabinet level" status (2009) * Note: Bush removed the EPA from this status

• Beginning discussions with Congress for comprehensive immigration reform (2010)

* Note: Much of Obama's immigration reform had been stalled by opposition in Congress

• Commissioned expert panels and reports from NASA; announced a new direction for human space flight that involves funding a new heavy lift-launcher and jettisoning the Ares 1 program; boosting NASA's budget by $1 billion in 2011 (2010)

• Ordered a ban on text-messaging for all commercial truck and bus drivers (2010)

BY THE WAY, DID YOU KNOW...

• The Obama Family paid for the renovations of the private living quarters in the White House with their own money rather than using the funds provided to all new first families (2009)

• The Obama Family reused many Christmas ornaments from previous White House trees rather than buy new ones (2009)

• The Obama Family used LED energy-saving lights on White House Christmas tree (2009)

• Awarded the Nobel Peace Prize; donated the award money for the prize to several charities (2009)

• Planted a garden for the White House's vegetables and flowers (2009)

• Installed a swing set/playground for the Obama daughters and children of White House employees (2009)

• Held over 150 public town halls, press conferences, interviews, etc. in first year in office (2009)
 Note: Official numbers are not available on such things, but this seems to be a new record high

• Less than 30 days of vacation in first year in office (2009)
 Note: Official numbers are not readily available on such things, but this seems to be a new record low.

MR. PRESIDENT 2012

There are countless reasons why America should re-elect President Obama:

Economic Improvement:
When Obama took the oath of office, the U.S. economy was in economic free-fall. It's far from the pink of health – but with 3 percent growth in the fourth quarter and 853,000 jobs created in in 2011's second half, it is getting better.

Foreign policy:
As Commander in Chief, President Obama has done an amazing job. He took out Osama bin Laden; he helped spur the NATO coalition that stopped Moammar Gadhafi; and he ended the Iraq War. And his use of drones to strike terrorist targets in Pakistan is a particularly effective use of our technology and intelligence to take out our enemies with minimal risk to American troops.

Corporate American Profit:
In 2010 and 2011, corporate profits hit record levels. Specifically, profits in 2010 were $1.66 trillion and as of August 2011, they were up 8.3 percent from 2010 – meaning that at that rate, 2011 profits totaled $1.8 trillion — setting a new all-time record as revenues grew 7 percent.

Stock market:
In the three years since he took over as President, the stock market has rallied sharply. On January 20, 2009 the S&P 500 index was at 832. Three years later, it had recovered to 1,315 – a 16.5 percent compound annual growth rate (the second best in the last 65 years).

A Man of Valor:

Often people complain about the President winning the Nobel Peace Prize. Personally, I think it's quite apropos! The President created a new climate in international politics and diplomacy. The President's cool, laid back and professional demeanor shows he is focused and committed to his cause. In essence, he has courage! He is the most courageous person in the height of battle that I've ever seen.
The truth is there are Americans out there who hate him and actually wish to see him dead! These truths are most unfortunate! The hatred he continues to encounter on a daily basis is probably unprecedented for any U.S. president in the history of America.. For example, in October 2009, The Boston Globe reported on an "unprecedented number of death threats (about 30 a day) against President Obama, there is a rise in racist hate groups, and a new wave of anti-Obama Administration fervor!" This is a man of true courage and valor.
Mr. Obama has spent his first term just trying to clean up the numerous gigantic mistakes that he inherited from his predecessor. He has succeeded remarkably well with little support, or even applause!

I think President Barack Obama deserves a second term in 2012.

Author's Note

Hello! My name is Azaan Kamau. I am a Choctaw Indian African American, originally from the tiny town of Madisonville, Texas! I am a nationally syndicated journalist, poet, independent publisher, and photographer.

I use my images, writing and publishing as tools to educate, empower, and uplift all people.

Thank you so very much for your interest in this little book of interesting facts!

Please feel free to check out all of the Glover Lane Press Publications of 2012!

For more information about me, my published books, my authors or the publishing company Glover Lane Press please visit:
http://gloverlanepress.webs.com
http://azaankamau.webs.com
http://letterstomybully.webs.com

VISIT ME ON FACEBOOK!

www.ingramcontent.com/pod-product-compliance
Lightning Source LLC
Chambersburg PA
CBHW060654280326
41933CB00012B/2185